SWU-NAP- 028

THE UNIFORMS OF THE BRITISH LOYAL VOLUNTEER CORPS

INFANTRY AND CAVALRY IN THEIR RESPECTIVE UNIFORMS 1798-1799

BY T. ROWLANDSON'S & R.ACKERMANN

SOLDIERSHOP PUBLISHING
BOOK on DEMAND

SOLDIERSHOP SERIES

AUTHOR

Thomas Rowlandson (1756 – 1827) was an English artist and caricaturist of the Georgian Era, noted for his political satire and social observation. A prolific artist and printmaker, Rowlandson produced a wide variety of illustrations for novels, joke books, and topographical works. Like other contemporary pre-Victorian caricaturists like James Gillray, he too depicted characters in bawdy postures and he also produced erotica which was censured by the 1840s. His caricatures included those of people in power such as the Duchess of Devonshire, William Pitt and Napoleon Bonaparte.

PUBLISHING'S NOTE

NOTE ABOUT BOOK PRINTING BEFORE 1925

LICENSES COMMONS

ACKNOWLEDGEMENTS

A Special Thanks to NYPL and other institutions for their kindly permission to use some images of his archives, collections or books used in our book.

Title: **THE UNIFORMS OF THE BRITISH LOYAL VOLUNTEER CORPS - Infantry and cavalry in their respective uniforms 1798-1799** . Plates of Thomas Rowlandson. Edited by Luca S. Cristini. First edition January 2020
Cover & Art Design: Luca S. Cristini. ISBN code: 978-88-93275385
Published by Luca Cristini Editore, via Orio 35/4- 24050 Zanica (BG) ITALY. www.soldiershop.com

THE UNIFORMS OF THE BRITISH LOYAL VOLUNTEER CORPS

INFANTRY AND CAVALRY IN THEIR RESPECTIVE UNIFORMS IN THE ART OF THOMAS ROWLANDSON
1798-1799

▲ A finest and expressive military caricature by Thomas Rowlandson

THE WONDERFUL WORLD OF THOMAS ROWLANDSON

Loyal Volunteers of London & Environs, Infantry & Cavalry, in their respective Uniforms, this book representing the whole and original manual, on military platoon, & weapons exercise in 87 plates Designed & Etched by Thomas Rowlandson, and printed in London by Rudolph Ackermann in the 1799 year. Every uniform contain a descriptive text to each color plate. Hand-colored etched title-page and 86 hand-colored etched plates, all by and after Thomas Rowlandson. Expertly and almost invisibly rebacked to style. A wonderful and large copy of this important work by Thomas Rowlandson, with early impressions of the plates heightened with gold and silver.

In this work, Rowlandson presents some of his most elegant and effective work in terms of pure print-making. The result is arguably the greatest of all military costume books, in that it ascends beyond being a mere record of uniforms to become an elegy to patriotism, an important social document and a cohesive work of art, all produced at a time of great national peril. The phenomenon of the Volunteer corps arose as a response to the perceived imminent danger of invasion by the French Napoleonic forces. Rudolph Ackermann notes in his introduction that 'At this moment, the enemy had advanced their best regulated legions to the shores of the British Channel; and for the determined purpose of spreading through our land such miseries as have already rendered wretched their own'. The British response was immediate and defiant, and Ackermann goes on to note that when the Loyal Volunteers of London were inspected by the King on 21st June 1799 the roll-call of Volunteers, manning 11 different positions, totalled just over 12,200 men. The present work serves as a record of that overwhelming show of loyalty, as well as of the uniforms of all the main Volunteer forces. In addition, Rowlandson pictures each individual in a particular drill position, the name and details of which are given in the engraved text beneath each figure.

The our collection are based on to the original plates, (entirely restored) collected by Dr. Hendrik Jacobus Vinkhuijzen, a Dutch medical doctor. Great and eccentric collectors of military uniforms of the late 19th Century. This collection is now property of NYPL of New York.

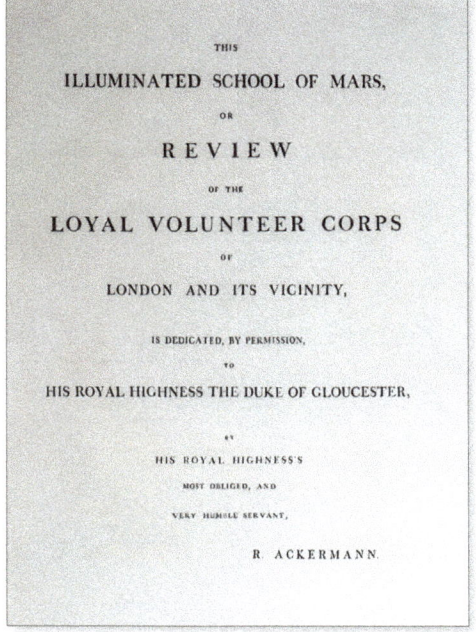

THIS

ILLUMINATED SCHOOL OF MARS,

OR

REVIEW

OF THE

LOYAL VOLUNTEER CORPS

OF

LONDON AND ITS VICINITY,

IS DEDICATED, BY PERMISSION,

TO

HIS ROYAL HIGHNESS THE DUKE OF GLOUCESTER,

BY

HIS ROYAL HIGHNESS'S

MOST OBLIGED, AND

VERY HUMBLE SERVANT,

R. ACKERMANN.

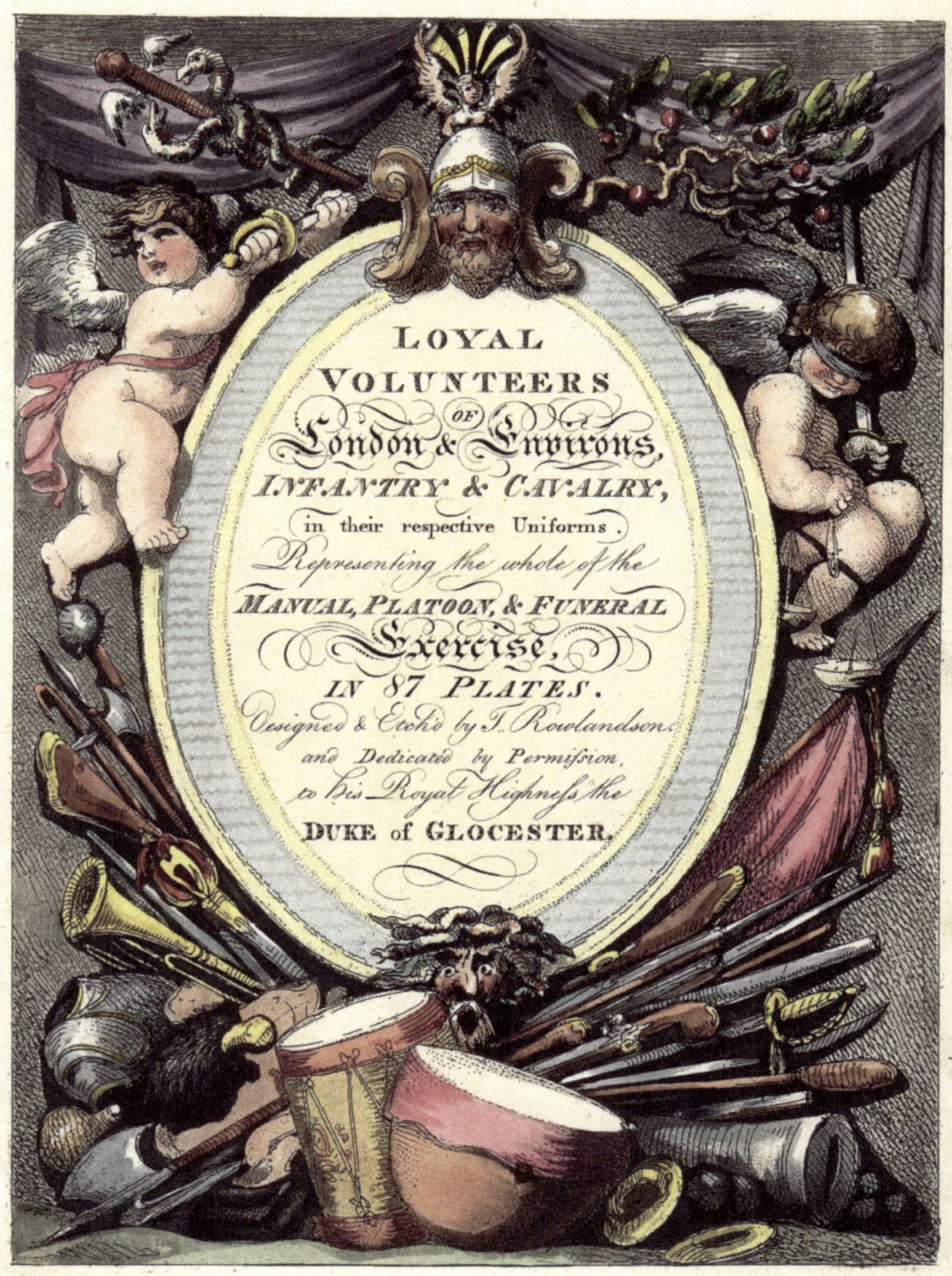

LOYAL
VOLUNTEERS
OF
London & Environs,
INFANTRY & CAVALRY,
in their respective Uniforms.
Representing the whole of the
MANUAL, PLATOON, & FUNERAL
Exercise,
IN 87 PLATES.
Designed & Etch'd by T. Rowlandson.
and Dedicated by Permission,
to his Royal Highness the
DUKE of GLOCESTER.

THE PLATES

St. JAMES'S VOLUNTEER

STAND at EASE

At the word *Ease*, the right foot is brought about two Inches behind the left, bending the left knee, & resting firmly on the right leg, the hands are shut in each other with the thumbs turned in. The piece resting in the right Arm with the muzzle against the shoulder.

Saint James's Volunteer

ATTENTION

*An Upright Position, the muzzle of the Piece placed in the Interval of the right Shoulder,
Right hand extended down the Sling. — Left hand straight down the thigh.*

London Pub. June 1798 at Ackermann Gallery N° 101 Strand

Westminster Volunteer

FIX BAYONETS *1st Motion*

At the word Fix the right thumb is slipt quick behind the Barrel, & the left seizes the Bayonet.

London Pub. June 1 1798 at Ackermann's Gallery N°. 101 Strand

Broad street Ward Volunteer

ST MARY ISLINGTON.
VOLUNTEER

Rowlandson Del.

FIX **BAYONETS** 2ᵈ _Motion_

At the word Bayonet _the Firelock is pushed a little forward, the left hand draws & nimbly fixes the Bayonet. Immediately resuming the Position_ Nº 5

London Pub June 1 1799 at Ackermanns Gallery Nº 101 Strand

Saint Mary Islington Volunteer

St. MARY LE STRAND.
& SOMERSET-HOUSE
VOLUNTEER

FIX BAYONETS. 5.ᵗ Motion

Immediately after the Bayonet is fixed the muzzle of the Firelock is drawn back & the right hand brought extended over the sling, standing in the same Position as N.º 2

London Pub. June 1798 at Ackermann's Gallery N.º 101 Strand

Saint Mary Le Strand & Somerset house Volunteer

LONDON & WESTMINSTER.
DISMOUNTED LIGHT HORSE
VOLUNTEER.

SHOULDER ARMS 1.st Motion

At the word *Shoulder* the right Thumb is slipt behind the Barrel laying tight hold

London & Westminster dismounted light horse Volunteer

St CLEMENT DANES
VOLUNTEER

Rowlandson Delin

SHOULDER ARMS 2ᵈ Motion

At the word ARMS, the Piece is at once flung to the left Shoulder, & caught in the left hand.
Keeping the Body 'square' & perfectly upright.

London Pub June 1 1798 at Ackermann's Gallery Nᵒ 101 Strand

Saint Clement Danes Volunteer

BLOOMSBURY & INN'S of COURT
VOLUNTEER

RECOVER ARMS

At the word ARMS, the firelock is by a quick turn of the left hand flung a little upwards, at the same time catching
it with the right hand round the small of the stock, & with the left above the lock placing the thumb of the left hand
straight up between the Barrel & Stock, & the little finger to touch the feather spring with the end firmly.
against the upper part of the left Breast: with Elbows close.

London Pub June 1 1798 at Ackermanns Gallery Nº 101 Strand

Bloomsbury & Inn's of Court Volunteer

ST GEORGES. HANOVER SQ.
LIGHT INFANTRY

SHOULDER ARMS from Recover 1ᵗ Motion

Pass the Firelock with your left hand turn it with the right, bringing it to the Shoulder & receiving it in the left hand with a firm Blow against the butt: keeping the right hand over the breech pin the thumb placed between the Barrel & Lock the cock resting on the point of the forefinger.

The 2ᵈ Motion is bringing the right hand down to the thigh & standing as Nº 7

London Pub. June 1798 at Ackermann's Gallery Nº 101 Strand

Saint Georges Hanover Sq. Light infantry

CHARGE BAYONET 1.ˢᵗ Motion

Is done by flinging & catching the firelock across the Body, with the lock turned to the front, at the height of the Breast, the right hand holding the small of the stock with the thumb straight up the breech pin the left hand holds the piece by the swell, the firelock slanting upwards

London 2nd June 1798 at Ackermanns Gallery N.º 101 Strand

Saint Martins in the Fields Volunteer

St. GEORGES. HANOVER Sq.
VOLUNTEER

CHARGE BAYONET. 1st Motion

The Firelock is at one motion brought to a nearly horizontal Position by half facing to the right, the right wrist a little below the hip. Pressing by the right mans Firelock.

Saint Georges Hanover Sq. Volunteer

TEMPLE BAR & St PAUL'S
VOLUNTEER

PRESENT ARMS 1ˢᵗ Motion

At the word ARMS the Firelock is turned quick with the lock to the front the cock
against the ribs not mooving it from the shoulder the right hand seizing the small of the
stock

London Pub June 1 1798 at Ackermanns Gallery Nº 101 Strand

Temple Bar & Saint Paul Volunteer

CORNHILL VOLUNTEER

PRESENT ARMS *2.ᵈ Motion*

or Bringing the firelock to the Poize

The right hand brings the Firelock to the Poize, the lock turned in front about the height of the mouth the
left firmly meeting the Piece with the fingers extended along the sling so the wrist upon the guard & Elbows close

Cornhill Volunteer

Rowlandson Delin.

PRESENT ARMS 3ᵈ Motion
or Bringing the Piece to the Rest.

The Firelock is by a quick motion brought down from the Poize to the extent of the right Arm with the cock turned to the left grasp in the right hand holding the piece by the small of the butt keeping the little finger out of sight while the firelock is brung very down the right foot steps close behind the left. The left hand quits the peace & firmly meets it when at the rest keeping the thumb between the barrel & stock the little finger to touch the feather spring & the left chiefly supporting the firelock

London Pub. June 1º 1798 at Ackermann's Gallery Nº 101 Strand

Temple Association Volunteer

BETHNAL GREEN, VOLUNTEER.
LIGHT INFANTRY

SUPPORT ARMS 1st Motion

At the word ARMS, the right hand seizes the Firelock at the small of the Butt, leaving
room between it & the lock for the left Arm, which is at the same time brought across the Body,
holding the Firelock tight, with the cock resting on the Arm

Bethnal Green Volunteer Light infantry

Remendeen Drin

SUPPORT ARMS 2.ᵈ Motion

The right hand is quickly brought to its former position, extended along the thigh

London Pub.d 1.° 1799 at Ackermann's Gallery N.° 101 Strand

Bethnal Green Battalion Volunteer

Rowlandson Delin

STAND at EASE Supporting Arms.

A resting Position of sentries. The right hand is brought across the Body to seize the small of the butt which is brought a little forward the right foot steps close behind the left the left knee is bent & the whole weight rests upon the right leg the fingers of the left hand are placed between the body & the right Elbow.

London Pub. July 1. 1798 at Ackermann Gallery N.º 101 Strand

Hans Town Association Volunteer

SLOPE ARMS.

At the word ARMS push the Firelock up towards the Shoulder as far as the guard will permit, at the same time lowering the muzzle without turning the butt.

Deptford Volunteer

ORDER ARMS 1.ˢᵗ *Motion*

At the word ARMS *the right hand is brought sharp to seize the Firelock at the top of the left Shoulder keeping the Body square & elbows close.*

Rowlandson, Delin

London Pub June 16 1798 at Ackermann's Gallery N.º 101 Strand

Westminster Light infantry

Rowlandson Delin

ORDER ARMS 2.ᵈ *Motion*

The Firelock is brought from the left Shoulder to the right side the muzzle close to the shoulder & the butt two Inches from the ground at the 3.ᵈ Motion the butt is dropped to the ground & the right hand placed along the sling the same as N.° 5

Artillery Company Volunteer

PIMLICO
VOLUNTEER

Rowlandson Delin

UNFIX BAYONET 1.ᵗ Motion.

At the word *Unfix* the right thumb is slip'd behind the Barrel, the same as Nº 6

Pimlico Volunteer

UNFIX BAYONET 2.ª Motion

At the word *Bayonet*, the muzzle is brought forward the left hand crosses the Body & lays hold
of the Firelock a little below the socket of the Bayonet at the same time unfixing the Bayonet with the
right hand as quick as possible.

Richmond Volunteer

COVENT GARDEN
VOLUNTEER

Rowlandson Delin

UNFIX BAYONET 3ᵈ Motion

The Firelock rests on the right Arm, the right hand returning the Bayonet to the scabbard bringing
it a little forward with the left hand the 2ᵈ & 3ᵈ Motions follow each other rapidly without Interval

London Pub July 10 1798 at Ackermanns Gallery N°101 Strand

Covent Garden Volunteer

EAST INDIA COMP.ᵞ
VOLUNTEER

AN OFFICER. SALUTING.

East India Company Volunteer

HANDLE ARMS

At the word Arms the hand is brought up sharp to the muzzle taking hold of the ramrod with the joint of the forefinger & thumb keeping the elbow close to the piece.

Bishopsgate Volunteer

BRENTFORD.
ASSOCIATION

GROUND ARMS 1st Motion

After handle Arms the firelock is with a sharp pace of the right foot turned lock inward the muz; so inclining a little forward waiting the motion for grounding.

London Pub.d ...... 1798 at J. Asperne Cornhill .... New Bond ...

Richardson John

Brentford Association Volunteer

Rowlandson Delin

GROUND ARMS 2ᵈ Motion

At the motion, the left foot makes a firm step out, the right hand at the same time quits the muzzle, takes the Firelock by the middle & brings it to the ground with the right knee upon the lock & the left hand straight down the left calf

London Pub. Jun.ᵉ 1ᵗ 1798 at Ackermann's Gallery N° 101 Strand

Fulham Volunteer

Novlandron Delin

GROUND ARMS 3° Motion.

Directly the motion is given the Soldier springsup nimbly to his former position, leaving the piece on the ground, & bringing his body front, by a short turn on the heels. To Take up Arms is only reversing the motions. London Pub July 12 1798 at Ackermanns Gallery 101 Strand

Saint Andrew Holborn $ Saint George the Martyr Association Volunteer

CASTLE BAYNARD VOLUNTEER

Rowlandson Delin

SECURE ARMS 1st Motion

At the word Arms the right hand is brought up sharp to the small of the butt with the thumb between the barrel & stock & the cock resting on the first joint of the fore finger

London Pub Aug.t 1 1798 at Ackermann Gallery Strand

Castle Baynard Volunteer

SECURE ARMS 2ᵈ Motion

At the motion the left hand quits the Butt & is brought smartly to lay hold of the firelock just above the shoulder

Finsbury Volunteer

NEWINGTON. SURRY
VOLUNTEER

SECURE ARMS 3ᵈ Motion

*The left hand brings the firelock down quick with the sling upwards, & the lock under the Arm
the right hand is at the same time dropped to its position along the Thigh*

Newington Surry Volunteer

Rowlandson Delin.

PRIME & LOAD 1ˢᵗ priming motion
Front Rank.
At the word Load the firelock is brought at once down to the Hip the same as the second motion of
charge Bayonet the right thumb throws the pan open & the 2ᵈ 3ᵈ & 4ᵗʰ motions follow each other rapidly

London Pub. Aug.ᵗ 1 1798 at Ackermann's Strand.

Knight Marshal Volunteer

PRIME & LOAD *2.ª priming motion.*
(Front Rank)
The right hand quickly opens the Cartouche Box & draws out a Cartridge.

London Pub Aug.ʸ 1.ˢᵗ at Ackermanns Gallery 101 Strand

Guildhall Light Infantry Volunteer

CHEAP WARD
VOLUNTEER

Rowlandson Delin

PRIME & LOAD *3.ª priming motion*
(Front Rank)
Directly the Cartridge is drawn. It is brought to the mouth & bit open

London Pub Aug.ᵗ 1798 at Ackermanns Gallery N.º 101 Strand

Cheap Ward Volunteer

PRIME & LOAD *of priming motion*

Front Rank

When the Cartridge is opened the hand is brought to the Pan which by a couple of shakes is filled.

London Pub. Aug.st 1st 1799 at Ackermann's Gallery N.101 Strand

Chelsea Volunteer

MARYLEBONE VOLUNTEER

PRIME & LOAD 5.ᵗʰ priming motion
(Front Rank)

When the Pan is filled the hand is placed on the hammer & the Pan quickly shut keeping the Cartridge between the forefinger & thumb.

London Pub Aug.ᵗ 1798 at Ackermanns Gallery N.º 101 Strand

Mary le Bon Volunteer

PRIME & LOAD 6th Motion.
(Front Rank)

Directly the pan is shut the right hand slides back to the small of the stock holding it with the three last fingers & keeping the Cartridge upright between the forefinger & thumb

Coleman Street Ward Volunteer

ST. PANCRAS
VOLUNTEER

PRIME & LOAD *7.th motion*

Directly the motion is given face a little to the left at the same time bringing the Butt with the right hand a trifle behind the left hip. The firelock turns in the left hand and is placed by the left in a nearly perpendicular position

London Pub. Aug.t 1.st 1798 at Ackermanns Gallery N.° 101 Strand

Saint Pancras Volunteer

PRIME & LOAD 1st loading motion

In this motion the Firelock is by the left hand dropped within two Inches of the ground, the ... ... the ... of the leg, the cartridge is brought to the muzzle & emptied by turning the back of the hand ... with the thumb on the ramrod

London Pub Augt 1800 at Ackermann Gallery 101 Strand

Cordwainers Ward Volunteer

Rowlandson Delin

PRIME & LOAD 2.ᵈ leading motion

The right hand strikes the muzzle & Immediately reep the ramrod between the point of the forefinger & thumb.

London Pub. Aug.ᵗ 30 1803 at Rd.ᵗ Ackermann Gallery 101 Strand

Saint Margaret & Saint John West Volunteer

PRIME & LOAD 3.º loading motion

The ramrod is half drawn straight close by the muzzle with the back of the hand turned forward

Lambeth Volunteer

ST GEORGES Southwark.
VOLUNTEER

Rowlandson Delin

PRIME & LOAD 4.ᵗʰ loading motion
The ramrod is quite drawn turned over the Elbow & placed about one Inch into the Barrel

London Pub. Sepᵗ 1 1798 at Ackermanns Gallery Nº 101 Strand

Saint George Southwark Volunteer

St SAVIOUR Southwark.
VOLUNTEER

PRIME & LOAD 5ᵗʰ loading motion

The Cartridge is rammed down halfway by bringing the hand close to the muzzle, holding the ramrod between the thumb & two forefingers

London Pub. Feb.ʸ 1798 at Ackermanns Gallery N.º 101 Strand

Saint Savior Southwark Volunteer

Rowlandson Del.ⁿ

PRIME & LOAD *6.th loading motion*
The hand slides to the Top of the ramrod binding it with the forefinger

Saint Olaye Southwarh Volunteer

PRIME & LOAD *last Motion*

When the Cartridge is sent down the ramrod is quickly returns the left hand raises the firelock & takes from the ramrod is the firelock is to the shoulder by the right hand holding the ramrod between the finger & thumb & the motion he right hand grasps after slightly striking the top of the muzzle the left flings the piece upwards & catches it at the heel. —

Poplar & Blackwall Volunteer

Rowlandson Delin.

A Light Infantry Man defending himself with Sadlers Patent Gun & long cutting Bayonet.

London Pub Sept 14, 1798 at Ackermann's Gallery, 101 Strand

Sadlers Sharp Shooters

Anderson Delin

MAKE READY *(Front Rank)*

At the word Ready the firelock is brought to the same position as Recover (see Nº 8) at the same time cocking it.

London Pub Sepr 21. 1798 at Ackermanns Gallery, 101 Strand.

Ratcliff Volunteer

Rowlandson Delin

PRESENT *(Front Rank)*

At the word Present the firelock is brought down sharp, the left hand holding it by the swell the first &
middle finger of the right hand are placed in the guard the left Eye is shut & the right looks along the
barrel waiting for the word fire.

London Pub Sept 8ᵗ 1798 at Ackermann's Gallery 101 Strand.

Union Wapping Volunteer

FIRE *(Front Rank)*

*At the word Fire the middle finger pulls the Trigger strong & the Firelock is
immediately drops down to the priming position the same as N.º 52*

Hackney Volunteer

BERMONDSEY
VOLUNTEER

Rowlandson Delin

FRONT RANK KNEELING. MAKE READY

At the word. Ready the right hand catches the firelock by the small of the Butt & the left by the swell of the stock. the same moment the right knee & the Butt are firmly dropped to the ground. the Butt close to the left foot; the right hand holding the lock by the hammer & cock

London Pub: Oct.r 5 1798 at Ackermann's Gallery N.o 101 Strand

Bermondsey Volunteer

S.ᵗ JOHN. Southwark
VOLUNTEER

Rowlandson Delin

PRESENT *(as Front Rank kneeling)*

At the word PRESENT. the right hand brings the firelock. quick up to the Shoulder. the left hand holding it by the swell. waiting for the word "Fire".

London Pub Oct.ʳ 8 1798 at Ackermann's Gallery N.º 101 Strand

Saint John Southwark Volunteer

Rowlandson Delin

PRIME & LOAD *(as a Center Rank)*

The same as front rank. Excepting the firelock which is held a little above the hip.

London Pub Oct'r 1798 at Ackermann's Gallery Nº 101 Strand

Langbourn Ward Volunteer

MAKE READY *(as a Center Rank)*

The same as a front rank with this exception the right foot steps out to the right, instead of being placed behind the left.

Saint Georges Hanover Square Association Volunteer

PRESENT / as a Center Rank /

The same as a front rank with this exception after firing the left foot steps close to the right; &
the firelock is dropped to the priming position the same as N? 52.

Saint Sepulcre Midd.x Volunteer

PRIME & LOAD *as a Rear Rank.*
The same as a front rank excepting the Firelock which is held close under the Arm.

Farrington Ward Volunteer

Rowlandson Delin

MAKE READY *(as a Rear Rank)*

The same as a front rank the feet uncoupled, the right foot steps out to the right & the left steps forward

London Pub Nov 1 1798 at Ackermanns Gallery 101 Strand

Aldgate Ward Volunteer

Rowlandson Delin.

PRESENT *(as a Rear Rank)*

*The same as a front rank the feet excepted which are in the same position as Nº 56
& the Body leans rather forward*

London Pub Nov 1 1798. at Ackermann's Gallery, 101 Strand.

Walbrook Ward Volunteer

Rowlandson Delin.

ADVANCE ARMS.

The 1st & 2nd Motions of advance are the same as the 1st & 2nd of present see Nº 12 & 13 at the motion the forelock is from the poize flung to the right side, & caught by the swell in the left hand, & at the Cock in ye right hand, taking care to place the guard between the forefinger & thumb, the cock resting on the other fingers —

London Pub. Nov. 16 1798. at Ackermann's Gallery 101 Strand

Clerkenwell Association Volunteer

Rowlandson Delin

ADVANCE ARMS (4.ᵗʰ Motion)

At the Motion the left hand quits the firelock & is dropped to its position along the Thigh.

London Pub. Nov 16 1798 at Ackermans new Gallery 101 Strand

Westminster grenadier

Rowlandson Delin

SHOULDER ARMS *(from advance 1.ª Motion)*

At the word Arms the right hand flings the firelock a little upwards & catches it by y.ᵉ small of the Butt, the left hand the same instant seizes it a little under y.ᵉ swell, the 2.ⁿᵈ motion is the same as N.º 13, & the 3.ᵈ as N.º 9

London Pub. Nov. 18. 1798. at Ackermann's Gallery, 101 Strand.

Bread Street Ward Volunteer

Rowlandson Delin.

CLUB ARMS (1ᵗʰ Motion)

At the word Arms the right hand quits the small of the Butt & strikes it keeping the thumb in the rear of the Butt the right heel is the same instant brought square with the other

London Pub Dec 20. 1798 at Ackermann's Gallery 101 Strand.

Vintry Ward Volunteer

Rowlandson Delin

CLUB ARMS (2ᵈ Motion)

The Firelock is by the blow of the right hand turned under the left Arm with the barrel in front the
right hand lays hold of the firelock close to the left hand the little finger of the left touching the feather spring.

London Pub Dec.ʳ 20 1798 at Ackermanns Gallery 101 Strand

Portsoken Ward Volunteer

Rowlandson Delin.

CLUB ARMS (3ᵈ Motion)

The left Elbow is sunk close to the side & the left hand seizes the cock & hammer between the forefinger & thumb.

London Pub. Dec 9ᵗ 1798 at Ackermanns Gallery 101 Strand

Saint Catherine's Association Volunteer

CLUB ARMS *(4.ᵗʰ Motion.)*

*The right hand quits the firelock in front & siezes the whole of the Barrel & stock behind,
with the back of the hand turned on the left Hip*

London Pub.ᵈ Dec. 20, 1798 at Ackermanns Gallery, 101 Strand.

Farrington Ward without Volunteer

Rowlandson Delin.

MOURN ARMS (1.ª Motion)

At the word Arms the right hand quits the firelock behind & takes hold of the small of the Butt.

London Pub Jan 1. 1799. at Ackermann's Gallery, 101 Strand.

Bridge Ward Volunteer

Rowlandson Delin.

MOURN ARMS (2.ª Motion)

At the motion the firelock is dropped with the muzzle on the toes the hands remaining in the same place as before.

London Pub.ᵈ Dec.ʳ 10 1798 at Ackermann's Gallery, 101 Strand.

Tower Ward Association Volunteer

Rowlandson Delin.

MOURN ARMS *(3ª Motion)*

The left hand quits the lock & lays hold of the heel of the Butt, & the right is placed
on the point of the Butt, with the chin on the right hand.

London Pu.... 1799. at Ackermanns Gallery, 101 Strand.

Christ Church Surry Association Volunteer

Rowlandson Delin

PRESENT ARMS *1ˢᵗ Motion from Mourn Arms*

At the word Arms, the hollow of the right foot is brought against the left heel, at the same instant the right hand takes hold of the small of the butt with the back of the hand inwards

London Pub Dec 1, 1798 at Ackermanns Gallery 101 Strand

Loyal Bermonsey Volunteer

Howard Brown Del.

PRESENT ARMS *(from Mourn Arms 2.ᵈ motion)*

At the motion the left hand quits the heel of the Butt, & lays hold of the forelock a little below the feather
spans the forefinger & thumb pointed downwards, at the next motion the forelock is brought to the 2.ᵈ
motion of the Present the same as N.º 14.

London Pub. Jan 1. 1799. at Ackermann's Gallery. 101 Strand.

Bhlinsgate Association Volunteer

Rowlandson Delin.

AN OFFICER OF THE HIGHLAND ASSOCIATION.

London Pub Jan 1 1799 at Ackermann's Gallery 101 Strand

Officer of the Highland Association

Rowlandson Delin.

PRESENT ARMS (2ª Flugel Motion)
The first & third Motions are the same as a Rank & Files

London Pub.ª Feb.ª 1. 1799 at Ackermanns Gallery 101 Strand

Whitechapel Association Volunteer

ORDER ARMS (2ᵈ Flugel Motion)
The first & third Motions are the same as a Rank & Files

Bank of England Light Infantry

CANDLEWICK WARD ASSOCIATION.

SUPPORT ARMS *(1ª Flugel Motion.)*

Candlewick Ward Association Volunteer

A SERGEANT with ARMS ADVANCED

Queenhithe Ward Volunteer

ORDER ARMS *(from advance Arms 1st motion.)*

At the order Arms the left hand is brought sharp across the Body, laying hold of the whole of the Barrel & stock.

Cripplegate Ward without Volunteer

ORDER ARMS (from Advance 2ª Motion)

At the Motion the right hand quits the Lock & smartly lays hold of the Firelock near the Trumpet &
at the 2ª motion the firelock is forced to the Ground the left hand quitting it & right is extended along
the sling the same as attent.

Dowgate Ward Volunteer

Nº 77.
MILE END
VOLUNTEER

Nº 78.
SHOREDITCH
VOLUNTEER

Nº 79.
TRINITY MINORIES
VOLUNTEER

PILE ARMS.

At the Command the Front Rank Nº 79, face to the right about & at the word Arms the front & Center
Ranks 79 to 78, throw their firelocks into the left hand the front & rear ... their ramrods together
& the center Ranks lock by passing their ramrods between All the locks are ... ...

Mile End, Shoreditch & Trinity Minories Volunteer

LOYAL ISLINGTON VOLUNTEER CAVALRY.

Loyal Islington Volunteer Cavalry

London & Westminster
LIGHT HORSE VOLUNTEER

Light Horse Volunteer

SURRY YEOMANRY.

Surry Yeomanry

DEPTFORD CAVALRY

Deptford Cavalry

WESTMINSTER CAVALRY.

London Pub July 1, 1798 at Ackermann's Gallery, 101 Strand.

Westminster Cavalry

MIDDLESEX CAVALRY.

London Pub.d Oct.r 1, 1798. at R. Ackermann's Gallery, 101 Strand.

Middlesex cavalry

SOUTHWARK CAVALRY

London Pub. Nov. 1. 1798 at Ackermann's, 101 Strand

Southwark cavalry

Rowlandson Delin.

CLERKENWELL CAVALRY.

London Pub. Nov. 1. 1798. ao Ackermann's Gallery 101 Strand.

Clerckenwell Cavalry

LAMBETH CAVALRY

Rowlandson Delin

London Pub. Nov. 1, 1791, as Ackermann Gallery (...)

Lambeth Cavalry

TITOLI PUBBLICATI - ALREADY PUBLISHING

POLISH SOLDIERS DURING THE NAPOLEONIC WARS
THE POLISH LEGIONS, THE ARMY OF THE DUCHY OF WARSAW AND THE POLISH IN THE GRAND ARMÉE
LUCA STEFANO CRISTINI
SWU-NAP-002

AUSTRIAN ARMY DURING THE NAPOLEONIC WARS 1813-1818
K.K.OESTERREICHISCHEN ARMEE
LUCA STEFANO CRISTINI - JOSEPH TRENTSENSKY
SWU-NAP-003

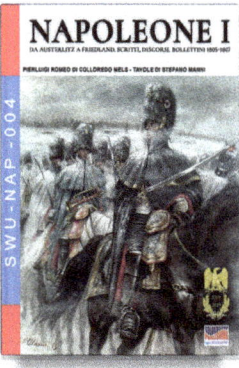

NAPOLEONE I
DA AUSTERLITZ A FRIEDLAND, SCRITTI, DISCORSI, BOLLETTINI 1805-1807
PIERLUIGI ROMEO DI COLLOREDO MELS - TAVOLE DI STEFANO MARNI
SWU-NAP-004

SPANISH SOLDIERS DURING THE NAPOLEONIC WARS 1797-1808
FROM THE VINKHUIJZEN COLLECTION OF MILITARY UNIFORMS
SWU-NAP-005

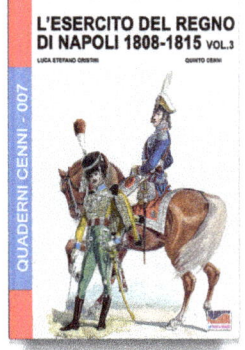

L'ESERCITO DEL REGNO DI NAPOLI 1808-1815 VOL.3
LUCA STEFANO CRISTINI   QUINTO CENNI
QUADERNI CENNI - 007

I SOLDATI ITALIANI CON NAPOLEONE 1796-1815
LUCA STEFANO CRISTINI   QUINTO CENNI
QUADERNI CENNI - 017

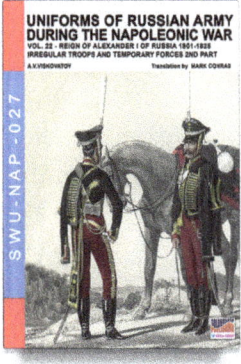

UNIFORMS OF RUSSIAN ARMY DURING THE NAPOLEONIC WAR
VOL. 22 - REIGN OF ALEXANDER I OF RUSSIA 1801-1825
IRREGULAR TROOPS AND TEMPORARY FORCES 2ND PART
A.V.VISKOVATOV   Translation by MARK CONRAD
SWU-NAP-027

UNIFORMS OF RUSSIAN ARMY DURING THE NAPOLEONIC WAR
VOL.21 - REIGN OF ALEXANDER I OF RUSSIA 1801-1825
IRREGULAR TROOPS AND TEMPORARY FORCES 1ST PART
A.V.VISKOVATOV   Translation by MARK CONRAD
SWU-NAP-026

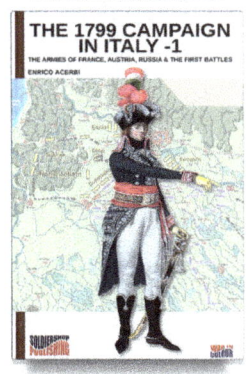

THE 1799 CAMPAIGN IN ITALY -1
THE ARMIES OF FRANCE, AUSTRIA, RUSSIA & THE FIRST BATTLES
ENRICO ACERBI

THE 1799 CAMPAIGN IN ITALY - 2
GENERAL SUVOROV'S ARRIVAL IN ITALY APRIL 14, 1799
ENRICO ACERBI

THE 1799 CAMPAIGN IN ITALY - 3
FRENCH ARMY AT ROME AND NAPLES AND THE TREBBIA BATTLE
ENRICO ACERBI

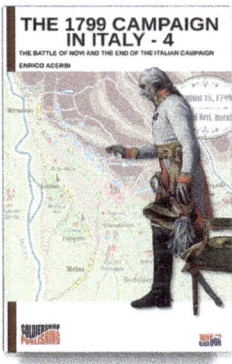

THE 1799 CAMPAIGN IN ITALY - 4
THE BATTLE OF NOVI AND THE END OF THE ITALIAN CAMPAIGN
ENRICO ACERBI

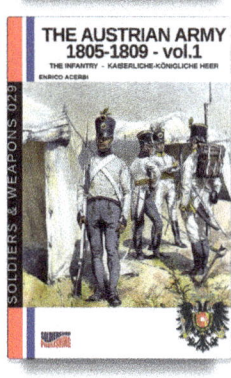

THE AUSTRIAN ARMY 1805-1809 - vol.1
THE INFANTRY - KAISERLICHE-KÖNIGLICHE HEER
ENRICO ACERBI
SOLDIERS & WEAPONS 029

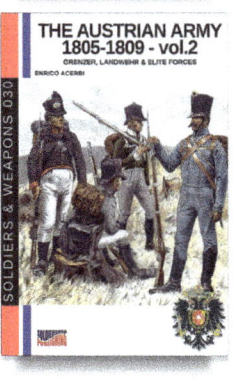

THE AUSTRIAN ARMY 1805-1809 - vol.2
GRENZER, LANDWEHR & ELITE FORCES
ENRICO ACERBI
SOLDIERS & WEAPONS 030

THE AUSTRIAN ARMY 1805-1809 - vol.3
CAVALRY, ARTILLERY & OTHER FORCES
ENRICO ACERBI
SOLDIERS & WEAPONS 031

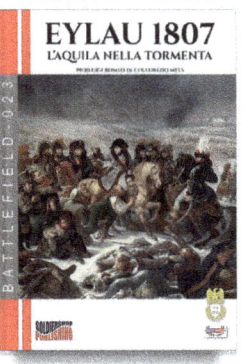

EYLAU 1807
L'AQUILA NELLA TORMENTA
PIERLUIGI ROMEO DI COLLOREDO MELS
BATTLEFIELD - 023

www.ingramcontent.com/pod-product-compliance
Lightning Source LLC
Chambersburg PA
CBHW041148120626
46547CB00020B/3149